THE PORTABLE DOONESBURY

THE PORTABLE DOONESBURY

BY G. B. TRUDEAU

Andrews and McMeel
A Universal Press Syndicate Company
Kansas City

"Things are more like they are now than they have ever been."

— President Gerald Ford

PART ONE
BIG TIME REAL TIME

"While you are away, movie stars are taking your women. Robert Redford is dating your girlfriend, Tom Selleck is kissing your lady, Bart Simpson is making love to your wife."
—Baghdad Betty, Iraqi radio announcer, to Gulf War troops

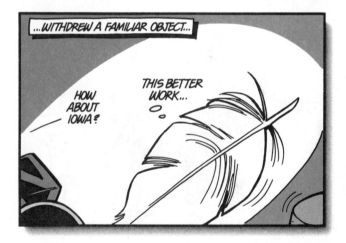

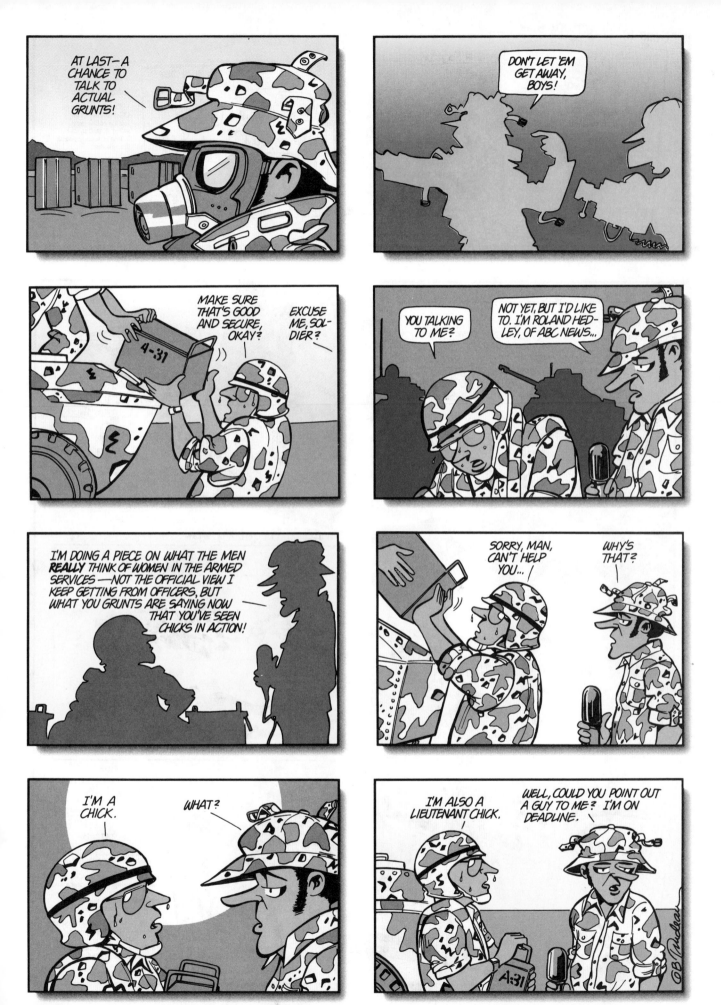

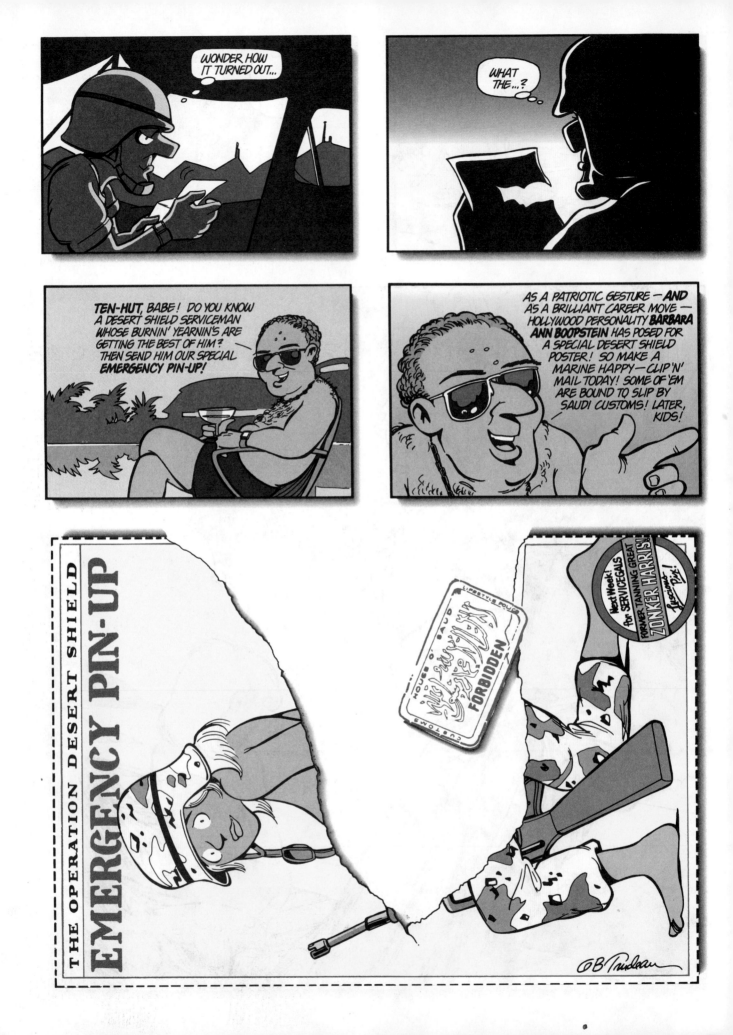

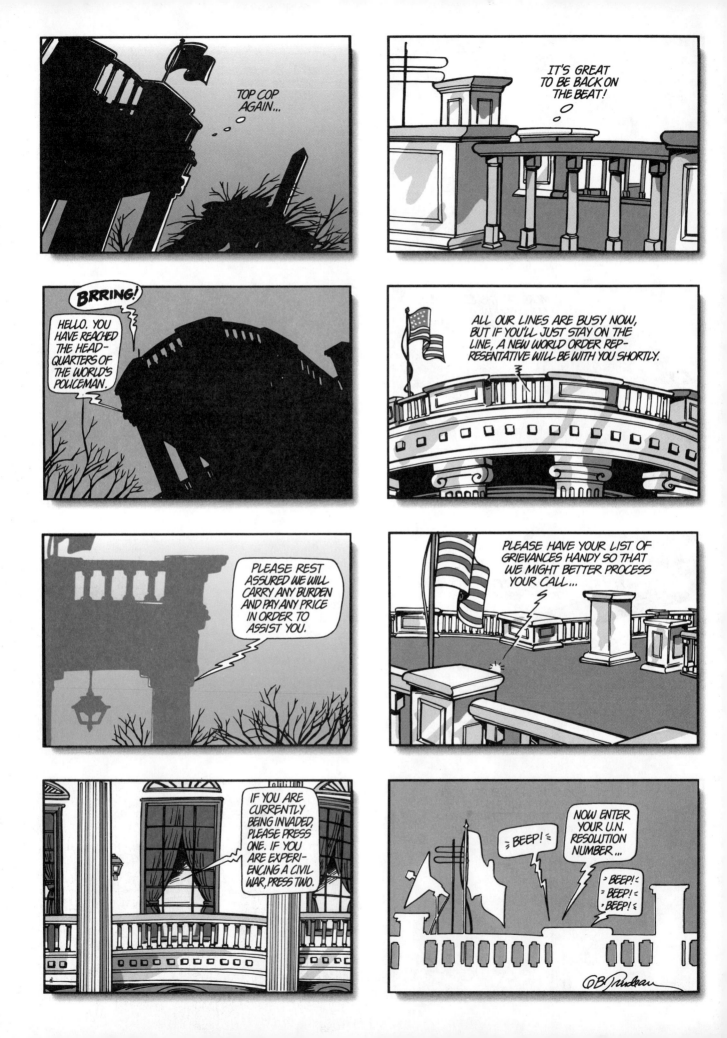

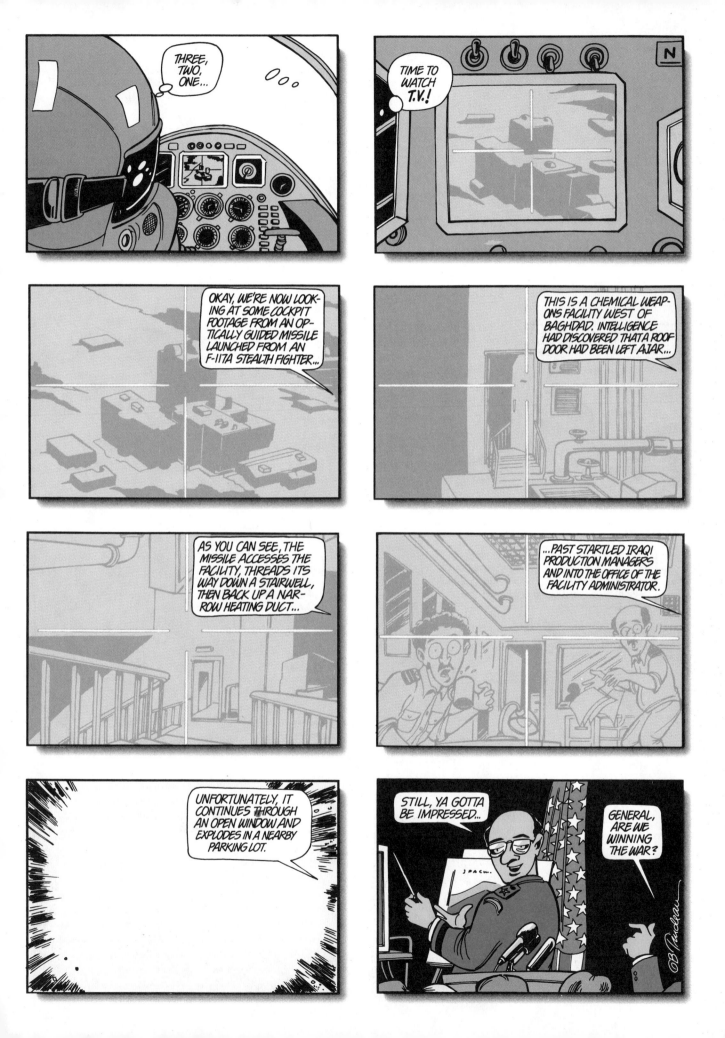

GOODNIGHT, BIG RED...

HELLO, BIG WHITE!

SERGEANT, TELL ME — DO YOU THINK THIS WAR HAS PRODUCED SOME LASTING ANIMOSITIES?

LASTING ANIMOSITIES? FOR SURE! IT'S GOING TO BE A LONG TIME BEFORE A LOT OF THE GUYS GET OVER THE MRE'S!

MRE'S?

MEALS, READY TO EAT — THE RATIONS WE WERE FORCED TO EAT IN THE FIELD.

I MEAN, I'M HERE TO PUT THE COMPANIES THAT PACKED THAT STUFF ON NOTICE — WHEN WE GET HOME, ME AND MY BATTLE-HARDENED BUDDIES ARE GOING TO FAN OUT ACROSS THE COUNTRY...

...AND TRACK DOWN EVERY LAST SUPPLIER! DITTO WITH THE PENTAGON PROCUREMENT GEEKS WHO BOUGHT THE STUFF IN THE FIRST PLACE!

SO THESE FOLKS ARE IN FOR SOME SERIOUS RIBBING, EH?

NO, NO, WE'LL BE PULLING THEM FROM THEIR CARS...

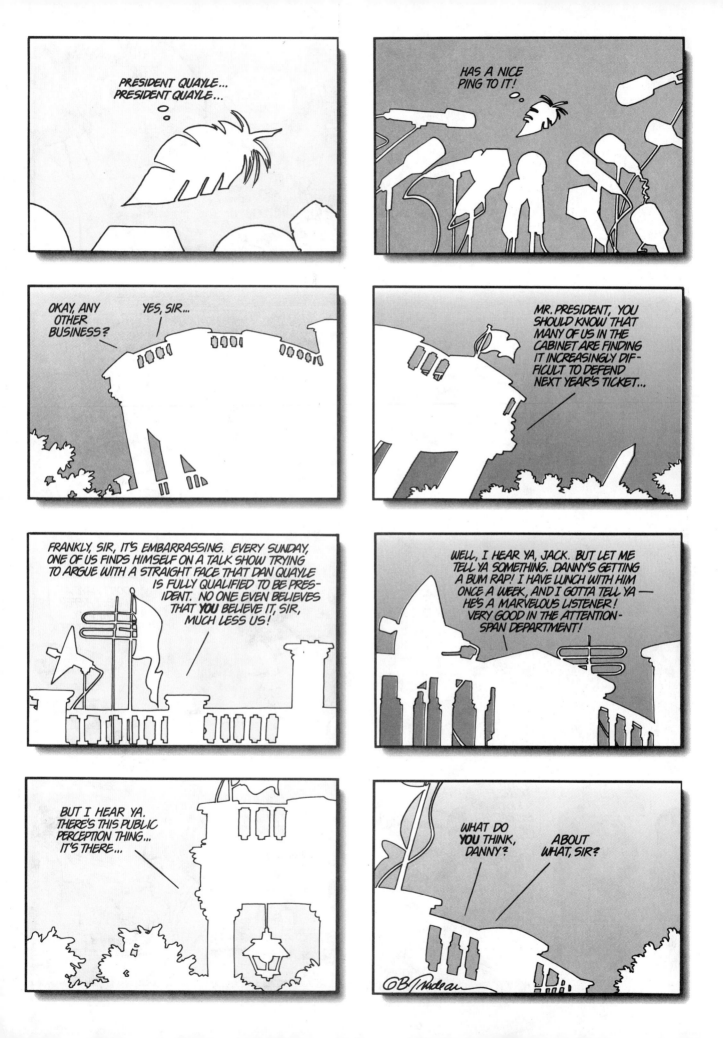

PART TWO
AIR APPARENT

"I love California. I grew up in Phoenix."
—Vice President Dan Quayle

SHOULD I SAY GOOD MORNING TO THEM?...

...OR IS THAT BEING INSENSITIVE?

GRADUATING SENIORS, PARENTS AND FRIENDS...

LET ME BEGIN BY REASSURING YOU THAT MY REMARKS TODAY WILL STAND UP TO THE MOST STRINGENT REQUIREMENTS OF THE NEW APPROPRIATENESS.

THE INTRA-COLLEGE SENSITIVITY ADVISORY COMMITTEE HAS VETTED THE TEXT OF EVEN TRACE AMOUNTS OF SUBCONSCIOUS RACISM, SEXISM AND CLASSISM.

MOREOVER, A FACULTY PANEL OF DECONSTRUCTIONISTS HAVE RECONFIGURED THE RHETORICAL COMPONENTS WITHIN A POST-STRUCTURALIST FRAMEWORK, SO AS TO EXPUNGE ANY OFFENSIVE ELEMENTS OF WESTERN RATIONALISM AND LINEAR LOGIC.

FINALLY, ALL REFERENCES FLOWING FROM A WHITE, MALE, EUROCENTRIC PERSPECTIVE HAVE BEEN ELIMINATED AS HAVE ANY OTHER RUMINATIONS DEEMED DENIGRATING TO THE POLITICAL CONSENSUS OF THE MOMENT.

THANK YOU AND GOOD LUCK.

JOHNNY? HI, IT'S MIKE DOONESBURY, FROM UPSTAIRS. YOU STILL HAVE THAT BIG GUN YOU SHOWED ME LAST WEEK?

OF COURSE, MAN. WHAT'S UP?

I WONDER IF YOU COULD GO OUT AND SHOOT THE CAR ALARM OFF THAT BMW PARKED OUT FRONT. IT'S HAD MY WHOLE FAMILY UP FOR FIVE HOURS!

SURE, MAN. HOLD ON...

GOT IT, MAN.

YOU'RE A GOOD NEIGHBOR, JOHNNY.

NO PROBLEM, MAN. YOU WANT THE HUBCAPS?

THE NUMBER YOU HAVE DIALED HAS BEEN DIS-CONNECTED.

HUH?

B.D., TOO?

ANY LUCK GETTING THROUGH TO MARK?

NO! AND B.D.'S PHONE IS OUT, TOO! I DON'T GET IT...

OH, NO... NOW **OUR** PHONE'S DEAD! WHAT'S GOING **ON**?

CLIK! CLIK!

CHANGING TIMES, BRO, CHANGING TIMES...

SAL! WHAT ARE **YOU** DOING HERE?

RELIEVING YOU, MAN. THE BIG THREE ARE OUT. IT'S TIME TO STEP ASIDE AND LET FRESH TALENT EMERGE.

YOU... YOU CAN'T BE SERIOUS! THIS FEATURE WAS **BUILT** AROUND US!

ANCIENT HISTORY, BRO. NOTH-ING LASTS FOREVER.

THE COUP OF THE SUPPORTING CHARACTERS.

MR. HARRIS, WEREN'T YOU DOONESBURY'S MOST **TRUSTED** ASSOCIATE?

HEY, I HAVE **NOTHING** TO DO WITH THIS! I'M JUST A FIGUREHEAD!

I **KNEW** THE KID COULDN'T BE TRUSTED.

YOU DON'T LOOK SO GOOD, ZEKE. YOU FEEL "ILL"? YOU LOOK "ILL."

BACK **OFF,** MAN! I'M **NOT** SHAR-ING POWER WITH YOU!

R-R-RELAX, FELLAHS! **I'M** IN CHARGE, CHARGE!

I'M NOT, BUT I'M **READY!** REALLY, REALLY **READY!**

TO BE CONT'D.

I CAN'T BELIEVE HOW **CLOSE** WE CAME TO BEING HISTORY!

IT MUST NEVER HAPPEN AGAIN!

MAYBE IF WE RETURNED TO OUR ROOTS...,

WALDEN? YOU? **HA!**

THE COUP, CONCLUDED.

HI. SINCE THE RECENT BOTCHED COUP OF THE SUPPORTING CHARACTERS, SOME OF YOU HAVE BEEN MAKING INQUIRIES ABOUT THE WELFARE OF THE EIGHT RINGLEADERS.

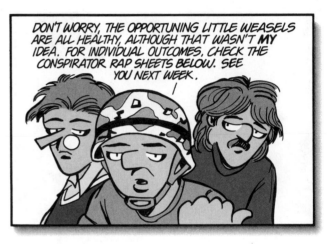

DON'T WORRY, THE OPPORTUNING LITTLE WEASELS ARE ALL HEALTHY, ALTHOUGH THAT WASN'T **MY** IDEA. FOR INDIVIDUAL OUTCOMES, CHECK THE CONSPIRATOR RAP SHEETS BELOW. SEE YOU NEXT WEEK.

THE PLOTTERS

AMBASSADOR DUKE: SUSPENDED FROM DAILY STRIP FOR SIX WEEKS. BANNED FROM COLOR SUNDAY COMICS UNTIL 1993. INELIGIBLE FOR INDUCTION INTO COMICS HALL OF FAME.

PHIL SLACKMEYER: PERMANENTLY BANNED FROM SUNDAY COMICS. STRIPPED OF SECURITY CLEARANCE. MUST WEAR ELECTRONIC BRACELET WHEN APPEARING IN DAILY FEATURE.

R-R-RON HEADREST: BANISHED FOR FIVE SEASONS TO LOCAL-ACCESS CABLE, WITH NO CHANCE OF RENEWAL. MAY NOT APPEAR ON ANY VIDEO SCREEN LARGER THAN 9".

JIM ANDREWS: STRIPPED OF STANDING IN NATIONAL SATIRE RANKINGS BY COMMISSIONER OF COMICS. ELIGIBLE FOR WALK-ON ROLES IN SPRING OF 1997.

ZEKE BRENNER: ORDERED TO SPEND THREE MONTHS IN A HALF-WAY STRIP, "ZIPPY THE PINHEAD." SENTENCE SUSPENDED IN EXCHANGE FOR FINGERING OTHER PLOTTERS.

SAL DOONESBURY: ALONG WITH DANO, BECAME "ILL" WHEN PLOT STARTED TO UNRAVEL. HAS SINCE DISAPPEARED; THOUGHT TO BE WORKING IN UNDERGROUND COMIX.

VICE PRESIDENT DANO: PLED "YOUTHFUL INDISCRETION"; BANNED FROM PLAYING GOLF DURING OFFICE HOURS. TRADED TO DISNEY FOR A CHARACTER TO BE NAMED, PLUS CASH.

ZONKER HARRIS: ENTERED PLEA OF INNOCENT, CLAIMING HE THOUGHT COUP MEMBERS WERE PLANNING SURPRISE BIRTHDAY PARTY FOR MIKE. CASE DISMISSED, DEFENDANT RETURNED TO PARENTS.

PART THREE
A GIANT, SUCKING SOUND

"They're trying to prove their manhood."
— Ross Perot, on two women reporters
who asked him tough questions.

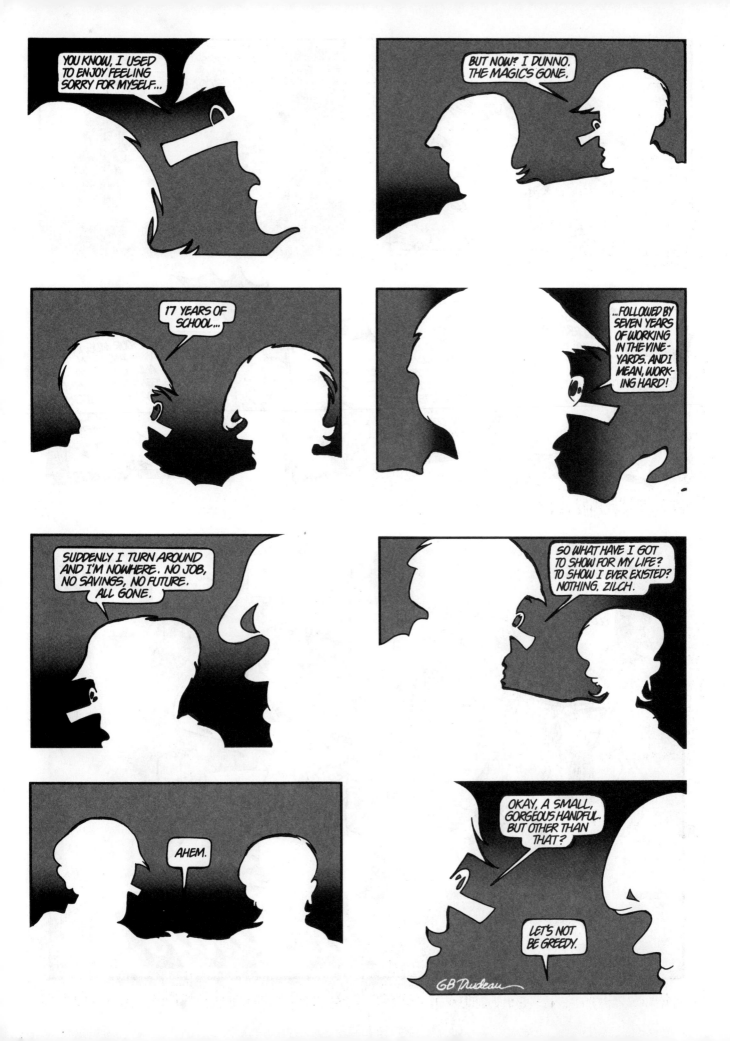

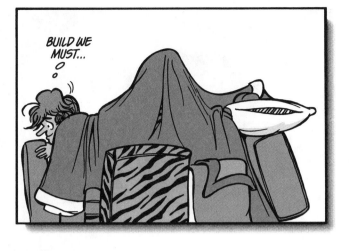

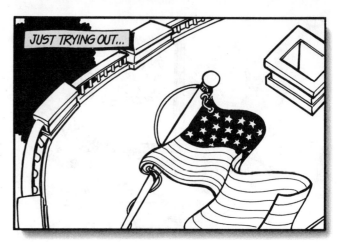

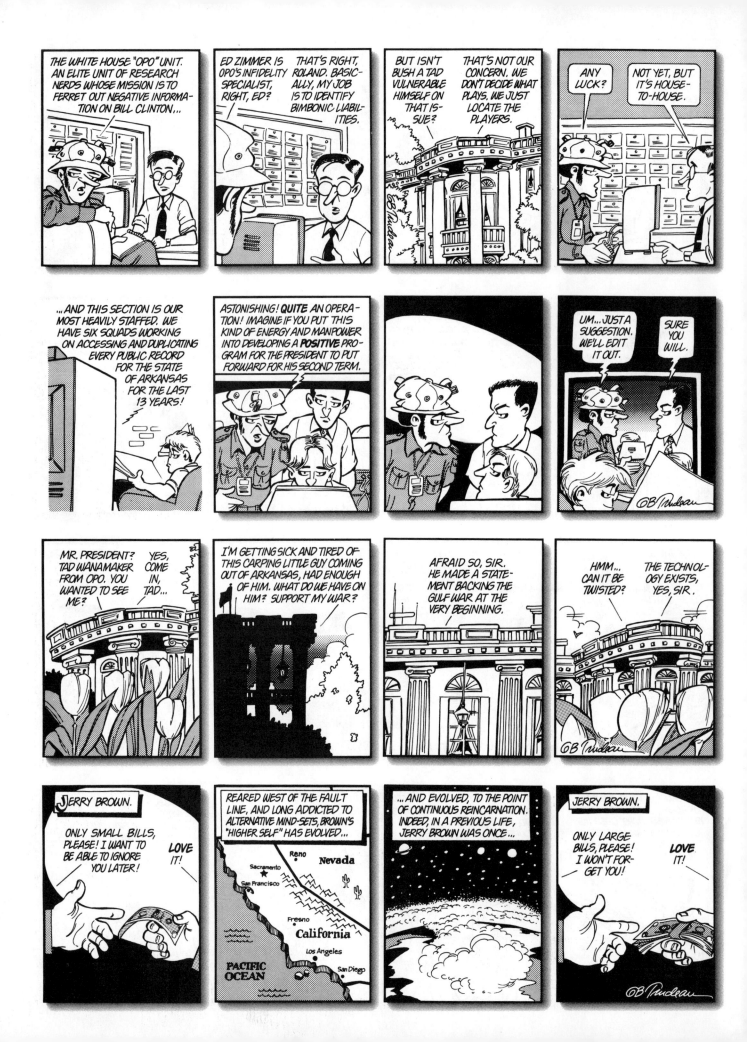

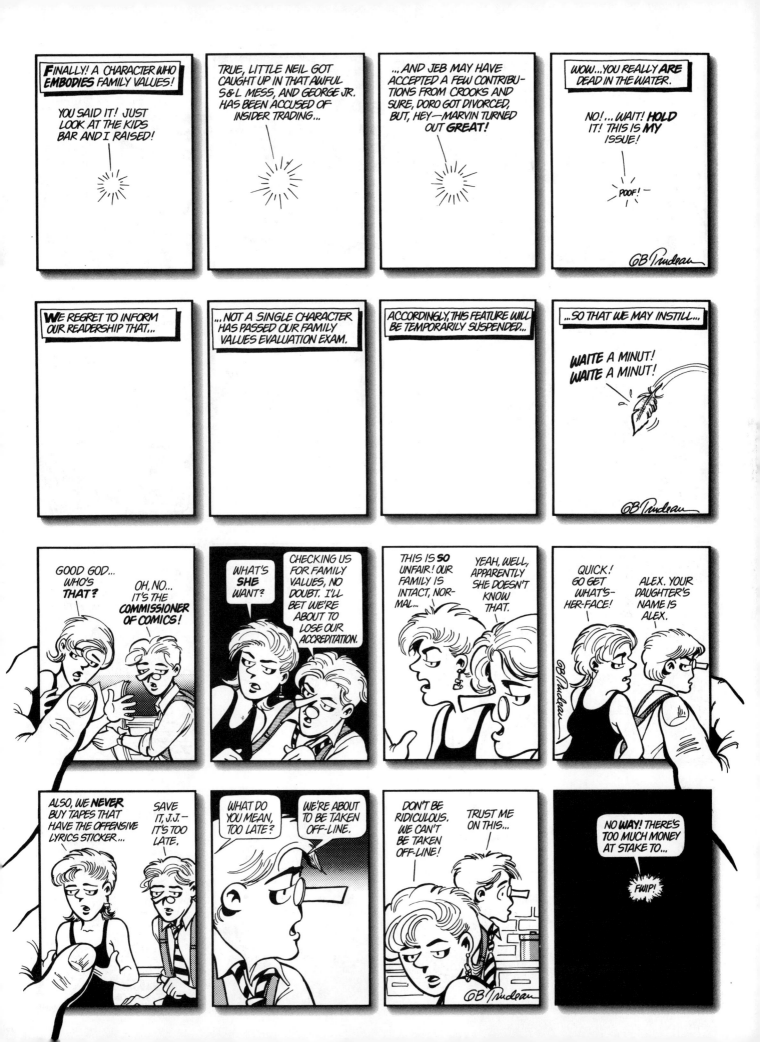

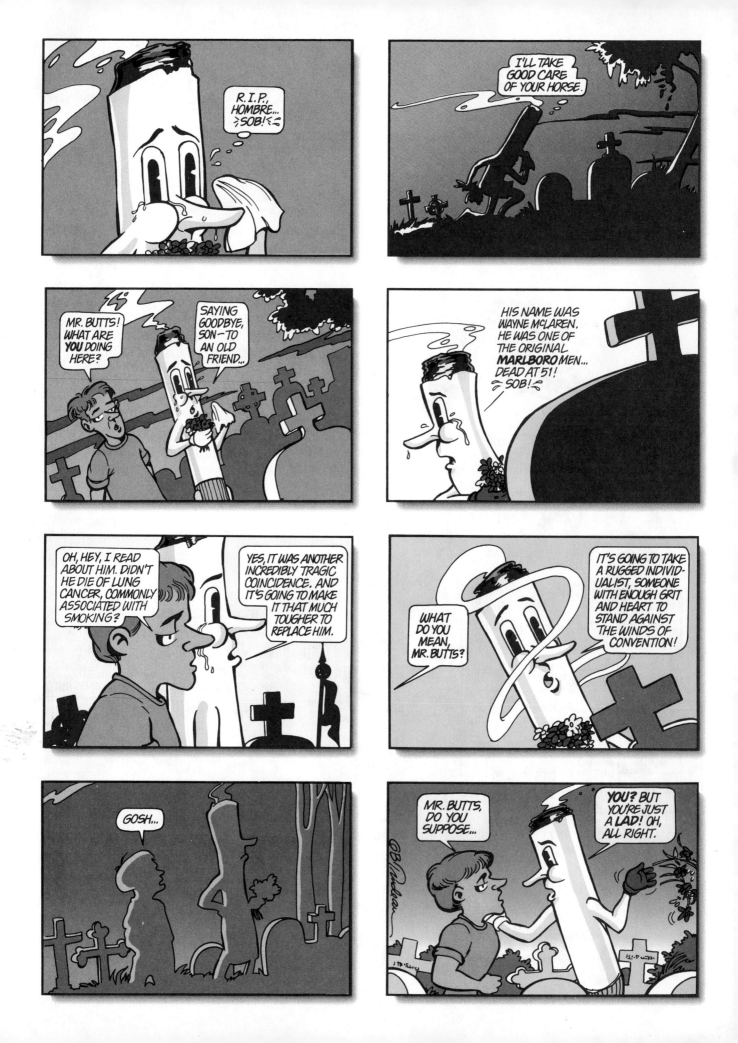

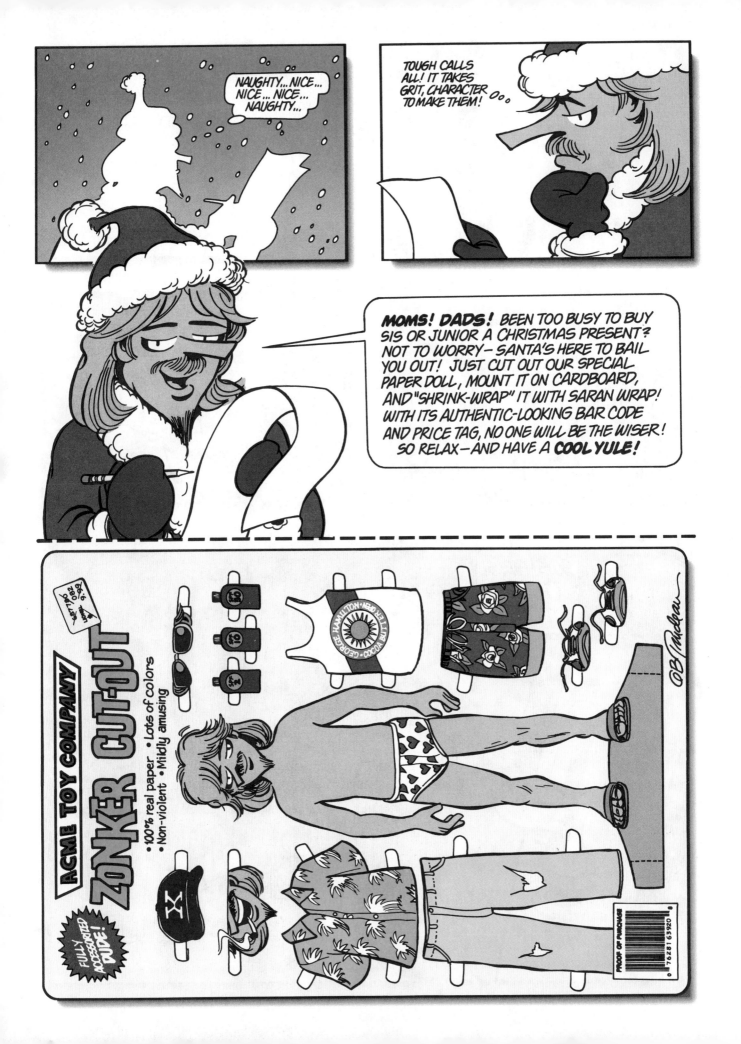

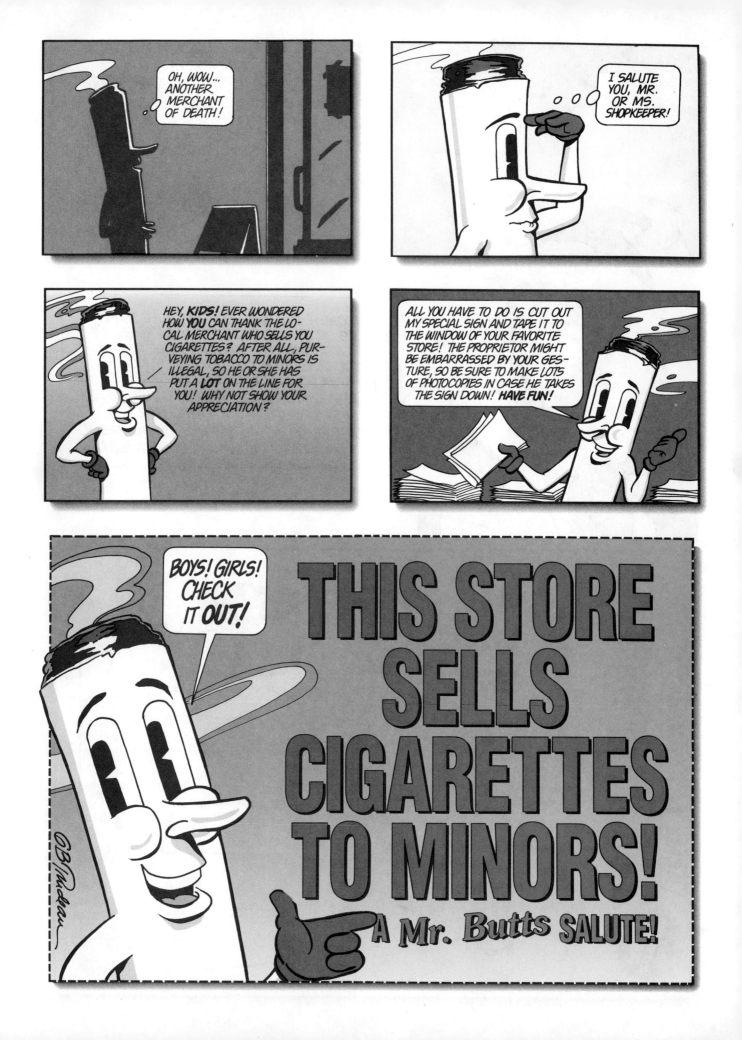

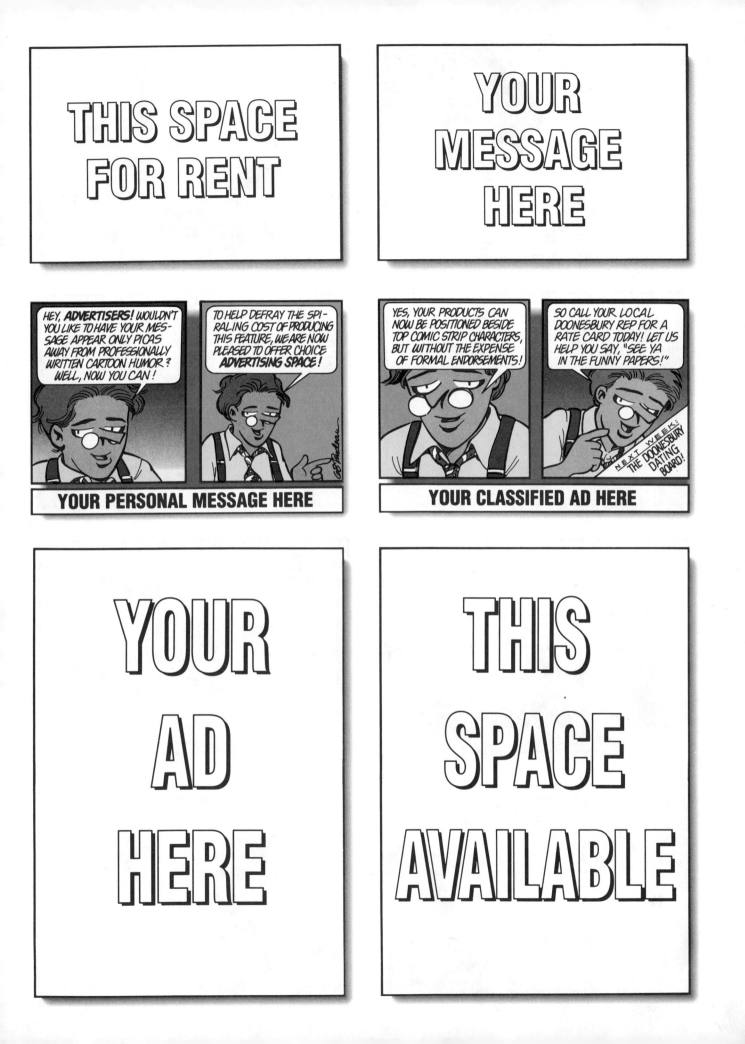

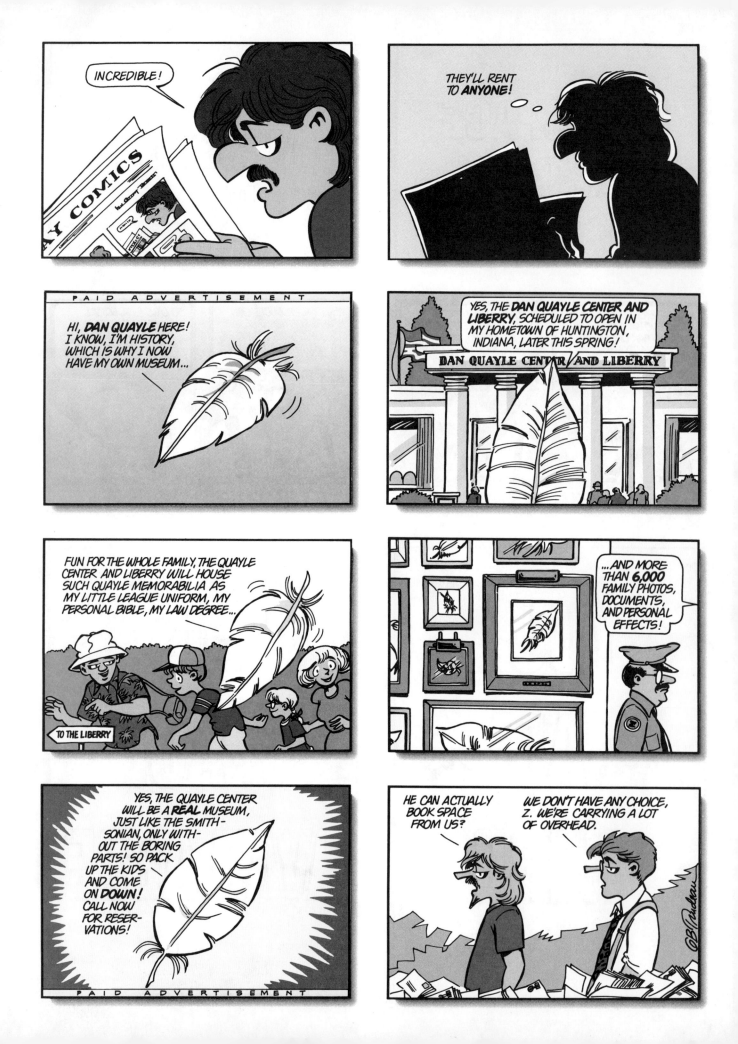

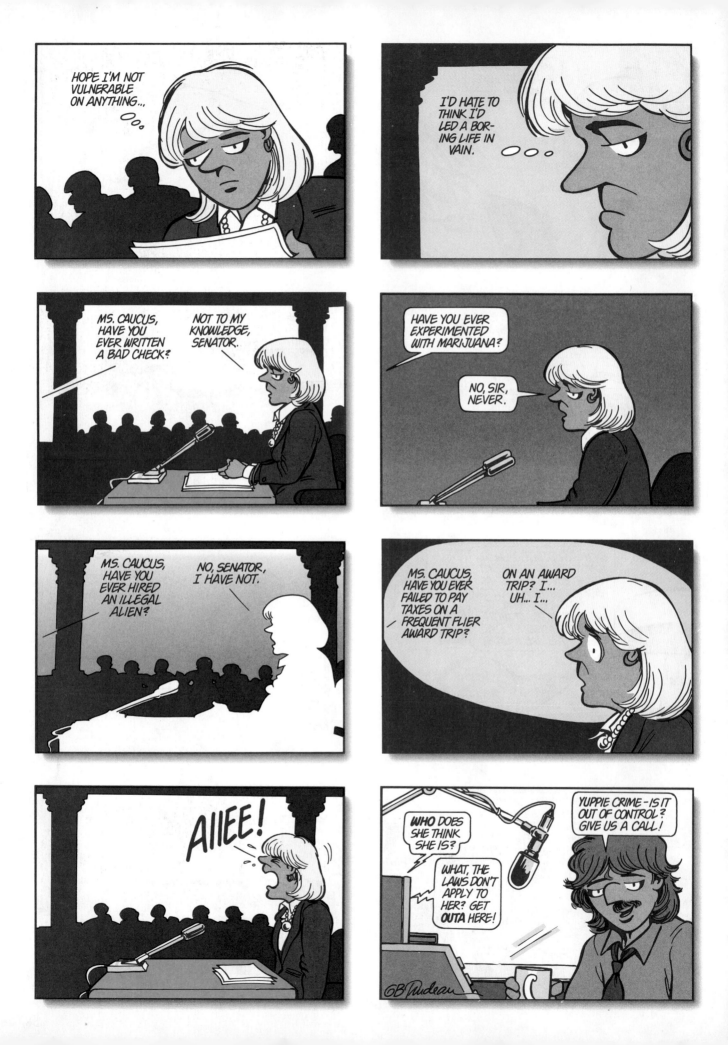